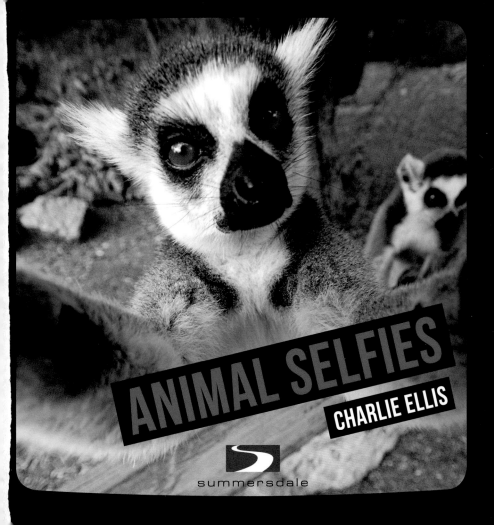

ANIMAL SELFIES

CHARLIE ELLIS

summersdale

SUMMERSDALE PUBLISHERS LTD
46 WEST STREET
CHICHESTER
WEST SUSSEX
PO19 1RP
UK

WWW.SUMMERSDALE.COM

PRINTED AND BOUND IN CHINA

ISBN: 978-1-84953-766-7

SUBSTANTIAL DISCOUNTS ON BULK QUANTITIES OF SUMMERSDALE BOOKS ARE AVAILABLE TO CORPORATIONS, PROFESSIONAL ASSOCIATIONS AND OTHER ORGANISATIONS. FOR DETAILS CONTACT NICKY DOUGLAS BY TELEPHONE: +44 (0) 1243 756902, FAX: +44 (0) 1243 786300 OR EMAIL: NICKY@SUMMERSDALE.COM.

TO...

FROM...

BE HONEST – DOES MY NOSTRIL HAIR NEED TRIMMING?

#LLAMASARETHENEWMEERKATS

WHY DO PEOPLE ALWAYS THINK THAT JUST BECAUSE I'M A CHAMELEON I BELIEVE IN KARMA?

#PHILOSOPUSS

GOT MY PERM, GOT MY CONSERVATORY. LET'S GET THIS 1970S FASHION TREND STARTED!

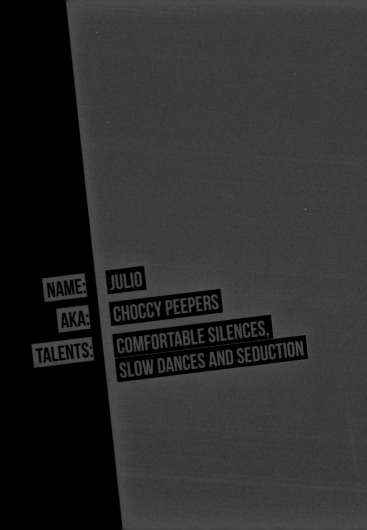

NAME: JULIO

AKA: CHOCCY PEEPERS

TALENTS: COMFORTABLE SILENCES,
          SLOW DANCES AND SEDUCTION

SINGLE BROWN MALE, LOOKING FOR A LADY TO TAKE ON LONG, ROMANTIC PACK RIDES AND SHARE MY CARROTS. MUST HAVE GSOH AND LIKE HAVING HER EARS NIBBLED.

#NOMAKEUPSELFIE

LET'S STAY LIKE THIS FOR EVER...

#YOUANDMEBABYFORLIFE

DOES MY NECK LOOK BAGGY FROM THIS ANGLE?

I'LL JUST WAIT TILL THE TIMER GOES OFF AND – OH NO, NOT AGAIN!

#THEORIGINALBABE

#WINNINGSMILE

QUICK SELFIE BEFORE THE STAG DO.

#GONNAGETCRAAAAZZZYYYY

NAME: PIERRE

LIKES: GNAWING HIS WAY OUT OF A CARDBOARD BOX

DISLIKES: PLASTIC BOXES

I THINK THIS IS MY
BEST SIDE, DON'T YOU?

WE LOVE A GOOD WALLOW.

#LIVELOVELLAMA

#LLAMALICIOUS

I AM HERMANN MEW PI,
AND THIS IS MY ASSISTANT,
KNOWN ONLY AS 'THE KID'.

#BFFS

HOW'S MY LIPSTICK LOOKING?

#TROUTPOUT

YEP, THAT GRUMPY CAT
JOKE IS TOTES ORIGINAL.

#SELFIENIBBLER

LOVING MY SHARP
DIOR BOB.

#LEMURSWAG

#SHELLFIES

YES, *YOUR* FACE IS
DEFINITELY WONKY.

I BOUGHT YOU FLOWERS
BUT THEN I GOT HUNGRY.

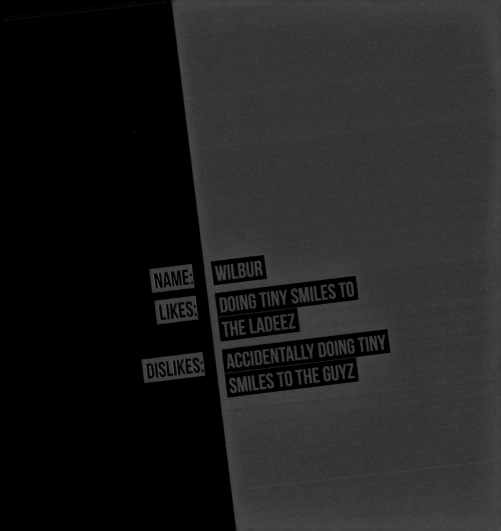

NAME: WILBUR

LIKES: DOING TINY SMILES TO THE LADEEZ

DISLIKES: ACCIDENTALLY DOING TINY SMILES TO THE GUYZ

#FADEOUT

#GLOW

#STREWTH

#NOTSOBONZER

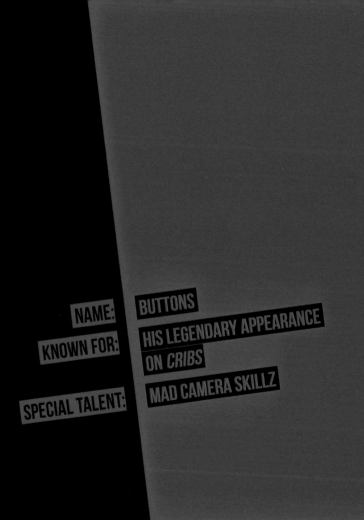

NAME: BUTTONS

KNOWN FOR: HIS LEGENDARY APPEARANCE ON *CRIBS*

SPECIAL TALENT: MAD CAMERA SKILLZ

#SOHORNY

NAME: CHAUNCEY

TALENTS: HAUGHTY REFINEMENT, DISDAINFUL BACK-TURNS, VOLATILE MOODS

THIS IS MY BEST
RHINO IMPRESSION –
WHAT D'YA THINK?

NAME: RED

DISPOSITION: CHEERY, UNTIL YOU CALL HIM A 'LESSER' PANDA

MY WHISKERS WOKE
UP LIKE THIS.

#SIDEPROFILE #SPINY #LOUNGELIZARD

'BELFIE' MEANS 'BEAK SELFIE', RIGHT?

#BIRDSOFAFEATHER

ME AND MY BOYS –
WE RUN THIS JUNGLE.

#PUPPYDOGEYES

PHOTO CREDITS

IF YOU'RE INTERESTED IN FINDING OUT MORE ABOUT OUR BOOKS,
FIND US ON FACEBOOK AT SUMMERSDALE PUBLISHERS
AND FOLLOW US ON TWITTER AT @SUMMERSDALE.

WWW.SUMMERSDALE.COM